LEGACY vs. LIKES

By **MIKE SMITH**

with **ANDREW NORMAN**

ISBN 978-0-9993306-0-9

Published by

Jostens, Inc.
3601 Minnesota Drive, #400
Minneapolis, MN 55435

JostensRenaissance.com

I'm not here to trash influencers, digi-stars, or people with enormous social followings. My goal with this book is to highlight the massive differences between talking and doing, between leadership and influence, between legacy and likes.

This book is for those who want to make an impact, not just build an audience. It's for you young people — or you young at heart — who want to stop wishing and talking about impact and start creating it.

It's for you "leadership kids" who want to be known for something more. It's for you athletes with a four-year window to use your sport as a platform, not a privilege.

It's for you kids who are still unsure who you are or where you're going, but who know it involves being part of something meaningful. It's for you dreamers, outliers, and misfits.

For those of you who dream of having large online followings on YouTube or Instagram, I hope this book helps you recognize the opportunity to use your platform for people other than yourself.

I hope this book changes the way you view yourself, your school, the internet, and the world. And I hope it helps you realize what you really care about.

This book asks a lot of questions. Use the blank space and margins to answer them. Draw in it, or take notes — do whatever you want. It's yours.

Just promise me one thing before you begin: Answer the questions honestly. Lying to yourself doesn't hurt me. This book is all about you. You're the one who stands to gain.

As always, thanks for giving me some of your valuable time. Now, enough with this awkward chapter that doesn't really count as one. I hope you absorb, and enjoy, my thoughts.

Let's get started.

Mike Smith

1

**WE ALL
KNOW
THAT KID**

I BELIEVE IN *dreaming* DIFFERENTLY.

If someone is already doing it, or it already exists, I find my own thing. I tell kids to do the same. Before you can though, you have to find what makes you, you.

As you're discovering that best possible *you*, the people around you have an enormous impact. What draws you to those people you call friends or peers or mentors? Is it their image? Or is it something deeper? You need to know.

I grew up in a simple house in Rapid City, South Dakota, the second-largest town in the country's fifth-least-populated state. We weren't a wealthy family, and my folks worked hard to make ends meet. I was a middle child of four and enjoyed pushing my parents' buttons. For example, in the sixth grade, I decided to run away from home because my mom didn't like the friends I was hanging out with. I left a note, stuffed a bottle of water and some Zebra Cakes (I love Zebra Cakes) into a backpack, laced up my sneakers real tight, and took off. I felt like top dog until the sun set and I realized I was on the opposite side of town with nowhere to go. I walked up to two high school kids making out in the grass and had to borrow fifty cents to use the payphone. I called my mom (crying) and asked to be picked up.

Now, my family was far from perfect. We had our struggles at times, like all families do. But I'm incredibly proud of our clan. Neither of my folks came from money or privilege. There were no rich grandparents, or anyone for my parents to call if they ran into tough times. They worked their butts off to give my siblings and me better lives than the ones they had growing up.

It was a good life for the most part. We were happy to be different. Because my mom is Jewish, my siblings and I are Jewish. This made us extremely rare in South Dakota, the state with the fewest Jews in the country. (There were only 250 in 2016.) But our neighborhood was incredibly diverse. It was full of kids our ages from all walks of life — from every race, background, and family dynamic. My street was a melting pot of perspectives and experiences.

I was thick as thieves with my two sisters and little brother. We ran through our neighborhood as a crew and always had the others' backs. My older sister was a punk rock chick who introduced me to all sorts of music, stuff most kids in my town hadn't discovered yet — Green Day, No Doubt, Nirvana, Rancid, Bone Thugs-N-Harmony, Beastie Boys, Wu-Tang Clan, Tupac, and Biggie. When I was a kid, I could think of no cooler job in the world than working at a record store or skate shop.

I dyed my hair crazy colors and always rocked my favorite band T-shirts. Being different from the people around me seemed normal in Rapid City. Having your own style was expected. It was cool to stand out. My siblings, friends, and I rode skateboards, practiced jiu-jitsu, played basketball and baseball, and generally just loved running around together. We were happy kids, and life was awesome.

Then, the summer before eighth grade, we got the news: We were moving. Some of you know what it's like to move in middle school — tough. I had close friends. I liked my school. I had regular activities and hangout spots on the weekends. I didn't want to go anywhere.

But I had no choice.

As kids in Rapid City, we didn't have to consider who we were hanging out with. About to start high school in a new town, it was all I could think about.

On Nov. 6, 1996, my family packed up and moved 322 miles south to Imperial, Nebraska. It was a town of 1,932 humans (95 percent of them white) outnumbered fifty-to-one by cattle. I'd moved from a community full of kids who had first-hand experiences with all kinds of cultures to a no-stoplight farm town where diverse influences came only via television or vacation. (You had to have a satellite dish to get MTV. We didn't have one.)

Walking into my first day at a new school — rocking purple hair, Vans, and a Green Day shirt — it was pretty clear I wasn't like everybody else. For the first time in my life, being different didn't feel good. No classmates or teachers overtly, intentionally made me feel out of place. It wasn't like, "Hey kid, we don't accept your kind here." It was subtler. It was the way kids asked questions about what being Jewish was, or why my siblings and I all had shaved heads. (Back "home," it was cool to shave words and designs into your head — not so much here.)

After one of our first days, my sister came home from school upset because a teacher told the entire seventh grade social studies class, "You see, everyone, Katie doesn't look like anyone else here, and she's totally OK with that." I don't think the teacher meant any harm. But she somehow failed to realize that being called out publicly for anything at that age can be devastating.

I had a lot of moments early on when I would start

talking about music or skating, and my new classmates would respond with blank stares. It felt like speaking into an empty room. Clearly, I care about different things than these kids, I thought. All of this was a drag on my confidence and self-esteem.

The desire to connect, and to fit in, is part of everyone's story. So I started tweaking parts of who I was: I took a bigger interest in sports and less in music and arts. I essentially traded my saxophone for a basketball, *Thrasher* for *Sports Illustrated*.

Slowly, I began to fit in more easily with the rest of the kids. But abandoning some of the things that made me different didn't feel right. I was looking for one person with whom I could connect and identify. I was starving to find someone who thought like I did. And I finally found him that next year as a freshman in high school.

"It was my first record label meeting ever ... I was very intimidated. It was very scary. And I just remember playing a song and [the label head] looked at me and said, 'There's already a Taylor Swift.'

"It hurt my feelings so bad, but he was right. That lesson for me was ... it's OK to look up to people and be inspired by them, but they're already there.

"You have to be you."

Kelsea Ballerini, singer/songwriter
from her episode of "The Harbor by Jostens"

We all know that kid — the one who walks into the room and everyone pays attention. They're the ones whose responses we wait for to determine how *we will respond* in various situations. If there's a party or an event, their presence dictates whether it's cool. They're the kids who seem to have a natural it-factor. They appear more confident, more aware, and bolder than the rest of us. From their style to their interests to their following — they just have "it." And "it" gets our attention. That person is an influencer.

We all know that kid.

I t's rarely just one thing that makes most **influencers who they are,** and that was true of Scoop. Scoop was a senior, and he carried a combination of confidence and recklessness that you could see when he walked down the hall in the baggiest jeans, a black Tupac shirt, big hoop earrings, bright socks, and skate shoes. He played sports, but he wasn't much of an athlete, which typically brought popularity in the school.

Instead, he was clever. He got his nickname from an unconventional column he wrote for the high school newspaper, which often challenged cultural norms and the establishment. He listened to music that wasn't on the radio. He hung out with kids who were already in college. He talked to girls from other towns, and he could even get them to show up to our parties. He was the central hub of his friend group's fun. He wasn't afraid to get in trouble or to speak his mind. Scoop rocked the boat, and people noticed.

I knew right away: This was my dude. He was a guy who helped set the vibe in our school, and many of the things he was into were the things I thought made me, me.

Scoop must have seen something in me that reminded him of himself too, because he started taking this little freshman under his wing. One day, he invited me to

his house to listen to music. Sitting on the old, green sofa in his room, he held up a CD I'd never seen before called *Fat Music for Fat People* — a compilation featuring some of his favorite punk bands. We listened track by track, dissecting each song. I soaked it all up and made mental notes of the ways he was describing the bands, so I could regurgitate it. Then, Scoop said something interesting: Pay attention to which bands are thanked in an album's liner notes. Checking out the artists who influenced the ones you're into is a good way to get introduced to cool music and to start the process of exploring its roots. That advice did more than just change how I discovered music for years (until Spotify, YouTube, and other services came along). It taught me an important lesson:

All influencers are influenced by others.

We all have that kid, or those people, who impact how we carry ourselves — our clothing, talk, dress, even the demeanor we hold with our friends, family, and teachers. For me, it was the senior across the street. And because I now spend an insane amount of time in high schools as a youth speaker, I know today's influencers are more likely to be found online.

The modern-day influencer isn't the kid walking the halls — it's the fitness model, the fashion blogger, van lifer, or vlogger with 100,000 subscribers on their YouTube channels. They're often getting paid by brands to make the videos or images you see on their accounts. That's right; brands pay professional influencers to post about their products because they want to influence you to buy those products.

As a culture, we've never had such access to athletes, artists, and celebrities. Not only do we see them on the stage, the court, and the red carpet but also choosing their outfits, getting their hair cut, posing perfectly in every situation, and tagging brands in the process. This visibility makes it easy to just copy how they dress, how they do their makeup, how they talk, and

BUILD SOMETHING BIGGER THAN YOUR PROFILE

what they think. (We all know that kid in high school who bought their followers, and their entire facade is an exact rip-off of someone they follow online.) If a lot of us were really honest, we mimic much of what we see from influencers.

Whether you live in a small town or a big city, an apartment complex or the suburbs, the people you surround yourself with or follow online have a way of influencing who you are, and ultimately who you become. And that can be positive or negative.

It's up to you to decide who has an influence on you and how you allow those influences to shape who you are. Are you going to follow trends, seeking likes and short-term gratification, or will you play the long game and build a legacy?

Questions

1 What is it about influencers that impacts people so powerfully?

2 What's an influencer if we take away their followers?

3 What type of "influencer" am I drawn to? Why?

4 Be honest: How many "influencers" do I follow, and how does that impact the way I think, talk, and act?

5 If I could switch lives with any of the people I follow online, who would it be and why?

Your challenge.

Go through your timeline.

Who are the people influencing you? How are they helping shape your story? What makes them appealing to you?

Are you a carbon copy of an individual or group of people, or do you have your own voice? Are you yourself? Be honest.

WHAT'S ON YOUR MIND?

People and stuff fill four roles in our lives: They add, subtract, multiply, or divide.

They *add* if their overall impact increases our happiness, friendships, and opportunities. They *subtract* if they decrease those things. People and stuff can also multiply positives or create divisions. Rarely is anything all good or all bad, so you have to look at the overall impact: Is it positive or negative?

You're in high school for a total of about 1,400 days. That might seem like a lot, but in the course of your life, it's nothing. Trust me: It will go extremely fast. It's your choice how you fill those days and what you allow into your life. I think you're crazy if you don't surround yourself with people and situations that impact you positively. If someone or something's overall impact is negative, you don't have time for it.

Kick it to the curb.

2

**WE DON'T
DO THAT
HERE**

I always struggled in school.

It wasn't because I had trouble learning or because I didn't understand the importance of education — far from it. The skills, lessons, and experiences we gain in school form the basis of who we all become.

No, my issue wasn't with learning; it was with the accepted route to happiness teachers pushed from Day One: good grades + good test scores = good college = good job = perfect life. I just didn't believe that *particular path* was for me. Deep down, I always knew I was going to approach life differently than my classmates.

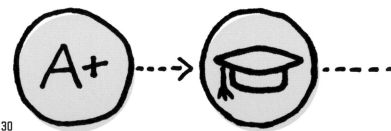

It was in my blood. My mom ran away from home as a teenager, ended up in a girls home, and ultimately dropped out of high school. But she went on to have a wildly successful career in corporate America because she worked super hard and has this gift for lighting up a room and making everyone around her better. For his part, my dad was a humble, thoughtful man who did whatever was necessary to take care of his family.

Neither of my parents graduated college, and they never demanded I go either. They just wanted me to graduate high school and do what I felt was best after that. So I never felt the same pressure most kids do today to get perfect grades. To me, school just felt like a necessary evil. This was my equation: pass classes + avoid major trouble = it will all be over in four years.

Starting college, I had never thought about growing as a leader. I viewed that stuff as a popularity contest in high school. Finding leaders to follow or learn from wasn't really on my radar.

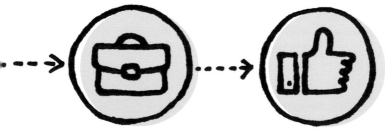

31

L ooking back, my only real motivation for caring about school came through sports. I made sure I did just well enough in my classes to stay eligible. Specifically, I wanted to play college basketball.

The odds of reaching that goal were definitely against me. When I was a freshman in high school, I was a half-pint with bright white hair (Eminem was at his peak) and tube socks. At just 5'1 and 101 pounds, I straight-up got tossed around like a ragdoll in the paint. I wasn't strong enough to shoot a real jump shot, so I developed a from-the-hip, gunslinger style. Despite my lack of natural ability, I loved the game and worked incredibly hard on my craft. By the time I was a senior, I'd gotten a little help — I grew ten inches and gained fifty pounds. Add hundreds of hours in the gym, and I was good enough to be my team's starting shooting guard. Though we made it to the state finals that year, and I had a good season, colleges weren't exactly lining up to sign this now-5'11, country kid with a 2.4 GPA and an ACT score of 18.

I ended up at a tiny Christian college of about 1,000 students in downtown Omaha, Nebraska. No one who played there was trying to reach the NBA. This was a school filled with kids who played purely because they loved it and wanted to be part of a team for another four years.

Here's an important detail to share: I'm a deeply passionate person. I don't do anything halfway. I live, work, and play hard. I'm a fighter, down to the last breath. When it comes to competition, I don't hold back — and not just with basketball. I'm talking everything: ping-pong, darts, cards. Everything is a contest to me. I talk smack, and back it up. I hold myself to a high standard, and I'm always my harshest critic.

When it came to basketball, I was known to let my passion (let's be honest; it was a temper) come out in colorful ways. I would chuck water bottles, yell at myself, mix it up with the other team, or even with my own teammates during practice.

When you're not the biggest or most athletic guy on the court, I figured you had to make up for it somehow. I brought extra heart.

But our biggest strengths often double as weaknesses.

During one of my first college practices as a freshman, I became really upset with myself after playing poorly. It was a pick-up game, and my team lost. After yelling a few words at myself you wouldn't say in front of your grandma, I picked up a basketball and punted it as hard as I could toward a nearby wall. As mad as I was at myself, it felt good to let off a little steam.

That's when I met John Jordan.

I had heard stories about the 6'6, lanky dude who could jump out of the gym and shoot the lights out. There were rumors he could have walked on at the University of Kansas (a college basketball powerhouse) and that the only reason he was even at our small college was because he followed his wife there.

John carried this mystique that made him seem ten years older, though we were basically the same age. Along with being married, he seemed to have life, and himself, figured out. Meanwhile, I could barely wake up for 9:00 a.m. class and ate tortillas filled with cheese and hotdogs for nearly every meal.

As a basketball player, John was old school. He didn't talk much or get overly excited. He rarely showed any kind of emotion. He played the game the way it was supposed to be played, with perfect fundamentals and a constant eye toward teamwork. He was head and shoulders the best player on our team, but he was also the best player in our conference and arguably one of the best in the country.

Simply put, John was a legend.

So that basketball I'd dramatically punted into the gym wall to show my frustration?

John wasn't having it.

He calmly approached me. He set his giant hand onto my shoulder, very stoically. And in his deep, almost fatherly voice, he said, "We don't do that here."

We. Don't. Do. That. Here. Five words said evenly that landed with brutal force. Then, he walked away without another sound.

I instantly felt small inside. I was incredibly embarrassed. I remember thinking, "This guy's in charge here, and I'd better learn from him." In that three-second interaction, I understood there were right and wrong ways to do things and that John Jordan was here to lead the way.

I realized I needed to do better.

Unlike some of the influencers I've known in my life, it wasn't John's charisma, style, or entourage that made me respect him. On the contrary, the dude never focused on the crowd or the hype. He wasn't a self-promoter. He never talked about how incredible his game was. He just put his head down and went to work, every day, consistently. John didn't have to walk into a room and tell people how hard he worked. The evidence was right there.

LEGACY

~~LIKES~~

> "The only way to have a lasting legacy is to **do something outside of yourself.**"

Azie Tesfai, actress/philanthropist
from her episode of "The Harbor by Jostens"

I remember one game where John played out of his mind: He went off, scoring a ton of points. As we returned to the locker room afterward, everyone was raving about his incredible performance. Instead of soaking in all his teammates' praise, John grabbed the stat sheet and began describing how well everyone else played. He pointed out how many rebounds our power forward grabbed, how many assists I dished out, and how the whole team locked down on defense.

John had every right to bask in the glory, yet he deflected the spotlight and took the opportunity to celebrate others. He showed me in that moment that **true leadership is about inspiring those around you in pursuit of a collective goal.**

John wasn't after "likes" — he had something bigger in mind: **He was building a legacy.**

John Jordan went on to be one of the greatest players that university has ever seen: He set records, single-handedly won games, earned multiple MVP awards, and was voted captain all four years of his collegiate career. He is also one of the quietest and most humble leaders I've had the privilege to know. This soft-spoken man of few words taught me more about what it means to lead than I ever learned from a book on leadership or from some class. There was no "10 Steps to Being an Effective Leader" when it came to John. He led by doing things the right way, working hard, and expecting everyone around him to do the same.

He led by example.

One of the things I appreciated most about John was that there was nothing fake to how he went about his life. He didn't live out some filtered version of himself — he was the same person on the court as he was in the locker room, on the bus, in the classroom, and at home.

Today, we often project what we want people to *think* we are, rather than offering up who we actually *are*. We hide inside the clothes we wear and words we use; we put forth a manicured version of ourselves in the photos and stories we share on Snap or IG. I learned a valuable lesson from John Jordan: *The best leaders don't live through a filter.* What you see from a person who truly leads, is what you get.

They are who they are — unfiltered.

Questions

1 How and why are leaders able to inspire people?

2 What kind of leader am I?

3 What is my first response when someone around me is successful? Am I happy? Do I get jealous? Do I enjoy celebrating others?

4 Who am I rooting for in life — just myself, or others?

5 Be honest: What is my true objective? Is it to impact others in a meaningful, positive way? Or is it something more superficial?

Your
challenge.

Choose three leaders from history: people who have accomplished truly remarkable things.

List the characteristics that made them leaders. Compare what makes them effective to the influencers in Chapter One.

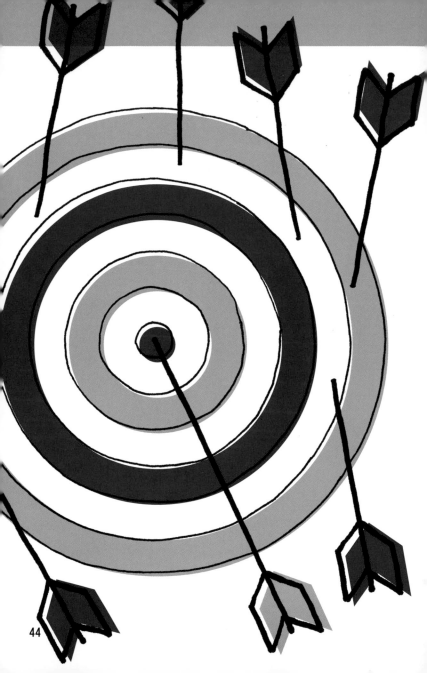

44

Have you ever noticed the difference between how leaders and influencers communicate online? I took a look at some recent tweets from individuals I'd consider either leaders or influencers, and comparing them is revealing.

For one, the leaders don't tweet anywhere near as often as the influencers: United Nations ambassador/human rights advocate Malala Yousafzai averages two tweets per day; engineer/inventor/investor Elon Musk tweets once a day on average; model/philanthropist Noëlla Coursaris Musunka tweets twice a day; and entrepreneur/philanthropist Jeff Bezos tweets once every twenty-eight days. Meanwhile, in the Kardashian family, Kylie Jenner averages six tweets a day; Kim Kardashian West tweets eight times a day; and Khloé Kardashian tweets eighteen times a day. YouTube personality Jake Paul averages six tweets a day, and Vine star Marcus Dobre averages eight.

Why do you think these leaders don't post as frequently? Perhaps it's because they're out in the world *doing* something. Their lives are defined by their achievements, not their personalities.

When they do post online, they make it count.

 @Leader_No.11  + FOLLOW

ROOTING FOR #TEAMUGANDA GIRLS IN THE WORLD ENGINEERING COMPETITION TODAY. SO PROUD OF YOU! #GIRLSINSCIENCE

 @influencer_208482  + FOLLOW

BACK IN L.A.

 @solar_leader_1 ✔ **+ FOLLOW**

I WANT TO THANK EVERYONE WHO ORDERED OUR NEW ELECTRIC CAR. WE KNOW YOU TOOK A CHANCE BUYING FROM A STARTUP. WE APPRECIATE AND WON'T FORGET IT.

$$\frac{ \rule{2cm}{0.4pt} \quad \frac{||}{VS.}{||} \quad \rule{2cm}{0.4pt} }$$

 @pop-star_7903 **+ FOLLOW**

TODAY WAS NUTS! THANK YOU GUYS FOR ALL THE LOVE OF MY AMAZING NEW FASHION LINE.

And what's the difference in who or what these leaders and influencers make the focus of their tweets? In the past year, Bezos' own face has appeared on his Twitter profile ten times. Kendall Jenner's has appeared sixty-seven times. Businessman/philanthropist Manoj Bhargava's face has appeared on his timeline five times in two years. YouTube celebrity Nash Grier has tweeted or retweeted pictures of himself 250 times this year alone.

Then, there's what they want from you.

LEADER

 @leader_No.11 ✔  (+ FOLLOW)

ONLINE AND IRL, I'M CHAMPIONING GIRLS. WILL YOU HELP ME?

$$\frac{||}{VS.}$$

Influencer

 @Follow_Me_73927 (+ FOLLOW)

HEY EVERYONE! WE HAVE NEW GEAR IN THE ONLINE STORE!!!

CLICK HERE TO SHOP

ORDER BEFORE IT'S ALL GONE!!!

LEADER

 @Biz_leader_15 ♂

I'M LOOKING FOR SUGGESTIONS.
IN BUSINESS, I INVEST FOR THE
LONG-TERM, BUT I WANT TO
START DOING GOOD TODAY WITH
MY PHILANTHROPY.

—————— VS. ——————

Influencer

 @Reality_Star_67892 (+ FOLLOW)

TAKE THIS CLICKBAIT QUIZ. ARE YOU MORE LIKE ME OR MY SISTER?

At the root of all great leaders is a craft — a passion they've hammered away at for years and years to become experts. (*More about this in Chapter Five.*) Take away social media, and these artists, athletes, humanitarians, and entrepreneurs are still leaders — their voices and impacts are still heard and felt, regardless whether they're on YouTube or streaming live. Take social media away from influencers, and what's left? Without you hitting that "follow" button, they have no power.

They have no reach.

3

**THE
SCREEN**

If you asked me when I was in high school (or during the first half of college) whether I spent more time trying to be an influencer or a leader, I would have said influencer, no question. I was more interested in building an audience than in making those around me great. I was influential with my teammates and with my classmates. I was confident and charismatic, so I could compel people to follow my lead in superficial ways: Friends and peers started adopting the way I dressed and started listening to music I was into. If likes, or being "Instafamous," had existed back then, I would have *lived* on my phone.

I also wanted to stand out and made it a point to be noticed. I remember telling a friend in high school, "As long as they're talking about you on Monday morning, you did your job." Today, that comment sounds so lame I'm embarrassed I ever said it, let alone believed it. Positively impacting my surroundings wasn't exactly my top priority. Still, coaches and teachers put me into leadership positions (perhaps viewing my ability to be influential as a stepping stone to leading). But for the most part, my behavior was self-serving.

That all changed my junior year of college.

Du: uring the previous basketball off-season, a bunch of great players transferred to our school. I'm talking a ton of talent for such a tiny university. That first semester, we were one of the top-ranked teams in our division. I thought our team had a legit shot at becoming a force to be reckoned with nationally. And if the first half of the season was any indication, I was right. This was going to be our year, and as a new upperclassman on the squad, it was going to be *my year* too. We gelled as a team, and we won a ton of games. When we all went home for winter break, I expected to return rested for my greatest-ever semester of basketball.

That's when everything turned upside down. Grade reports from first semester came out, and we lost half of our best players. Some of our team didn't pass enough classes to be eligible, and others had failed drug tests. It was as if this incredible team we put together first semester had just collapsed, and I knew we were in big trouble.

To keep our season from sinking, someone had to do something. And as the team's point guard and captain, I was too committed to take a back seat.

When you play basketball at a small college and you lose players, it's not like guys are just waiting on the bench ready to hop into the game. We had no redshirt freshmen. There was no JV team to call up. We basically had to go hunting for kids at our college who "used to play in high school." We were a little, blue-collar school with a lot of farm kids, pastors' sons, and small-town guys who worked hard and loved the game but were rarely incredible players. We needed more bodies to fill out our roster. We didn't have much time, and we couldn't be too picky.

So some teammates and I started going to intramural games and making a list of all the players we thought were good enough to join the team. We found a scrappy, left-handed point guard. We snagged a 6'3 forward who played tough and wasn't afraid to go after rebounds. One by one, we started asking if these guys wanted to play on our team. And they were saying yes. We almost had the roster filled, but we needed one more guy.

We settled on Wade Howard — a soft-spoken, soft-bodied Kansas kid with a silly personality. Wade was familiar with basketball but lacked much pure talent. He agreed to sign up for the team, but we needed him to actually *perform*.

I quickly realized while running a few drills during Wade's first practice that he didn't care about the game the same way I did. For him, being on the team was the end goal — not winning, not taking our team further than it had ever gone before. He seemed to just go through the motions. I *needed* him to care; I needed him to put it all on the line because I wanted to win. This was *my* team. This was *my* year. I had put in my thousands of hours in the gym. I had sacrificed late nights and early mornings to get to this point, and I wanted everyone to want this as badly as I did.

To me, basketball was almost life or death. It wasn't because I thought I was going to make it to the NBA or something — there was no chance of that happening. I had a passion for teamwork, for the experience of being on the court. And this was one of my last seasons to see how far we could go.

"What if we stopped caring so much about a reputation we have for four years and started caring more about the legacy we'll leave for 100?"

Scott Backovich, speaker
from his episode of "The Harbor by Jostens"

I wanted not just Wade but everyone on the team to have the same passion for the game. But during this period, I learned a valuable lesson: **You can't expect people to care as much about your goals as you do.**

We all have something that drives us. We all have that thing that makes us want to get out of bed and be better. For some of you, it's sports. For others, it's your community, or it's family, or art, or music, or dance, or dating. Some of you are working on earth-shattering stuff. Some of you are just stoked to beat the next level of a video game. Some of you haven't found that driving force yet (don't worry — keep reading). For some of you, your passion will be *finding* your passion.

But remember, you can't force your passion on others.

That semester, I was driven to play for a national championship. I wanted our team to be one of the best that ever played at that university. For that to happen, every player was going to have an important role. So I spent the first few weeks of that semester trying to figure out Wade's passion: What made this guy tick? How could I get him to perform?

In one practice, I finally discovered it.

Wade set a screen (you know, when you suddenly block a teammate's defender so they can go around you) that straight laid a kid out — absolutely knocked him off his feet. In that moment, as the defender struggled to pick himself up off the ground, I realized this was my opportunity to celebrate Wade. I walked up, grabbed him by the back of the head, and with my face full of raw emotion and intensity, I looked him dead in the eyes and said, "I have never seen anyone set a screen that incredible in my entire life. If you do that every game — every opportunity you get — you're going to make a huge impact on this team."

You better believe that worked. Wade's eyes lit up, and it was as if I'd unlocked the door to the one thing he believed he could do really well: be an immovable brick wall on the basketball court.

And that's exactly what he did.

Every time Wade got into a game, his entire focus was on setting the most vicious screen he possibly could. And he excelled at it — he turned into one of the greatest screeners I've ever played with in my life. In the game, his big blue eyes, which were normally soft and kind, would get really wide and serious. He'd look at whoever was guarding me like they'd just insulted his mother, and he would set the most destructive (sometimes illegal) screen.

Have you ever heard of a basketball player known specifically for setting screens? Of course not. It's a selfless act. You're putting your body on the line to help someone else score a basket. Screens rarely make highlight reels. They don't keep stats on it. But setting a great screen is a winning play, and all of a sudden, Wade was helping us win. He was making everyone around him better because I had committed in that one practice to letting him know he could.

The effect I had on Wade made me realize celebrating the small things people do well — the things no one else may notice — can help people, teams, families, and communities become greater versions of themselves. It also taught me to *look* for those opportunities. You have to pay attention. Maybe it's how another person listens, the way they encourage others, or the way they work hard when

MAKE EVERYONE

AROUND YOU

BETTER

no one is looking. **Sometimes celebrating the little things makes the biggest difference.**

Our team went on to win a regional championship, and we played in (and came close to winning) our university's first-ever national championship game. I remember being in the locker room before the game, looking around at this ragtag team and realizing we'd only gotten there because everyone out-performed expectations. I will never forget how we took a bunch of small-town kids from different parts of the Midwest and grew stronger as one family.

Until that season, I had just been influential.

That year, I learned how to lead.

I was voted a first-team All-American and our team's MVP. But I wasn't our team's best player, and I didn't put up the best stats either. That taught me *you don't have to be the best to lead, but you do have to be willing to take some risks*. Leadership isn't a rank, and it's not about authority. It's about making people feel safe to take those same risks in your presence and be empowered to be great, even through the small things.

I learned another lesson that season: You can be both influential *and* a leader. **But the people who have the greatest impact in this world focus more on leading than influencing.**

I've taken that same mentality into everything I do, from starting companies to founding a nonprofit. I believe I've succeeded because, rather than focusing on gaining followers or being influential, I spend time empowering and celebrating my team. I give my people opportunities and space to succeed, to fail, and to stand in the spotlight. My team always creates something bigger and better than I ever could on my own. I couldn't be more hyped on them and the amazing things we have done together.

From sports teams to successful companies, leaders of thriving collectives put the attention on their fellow team members. That's what leaders do — they celebrate others, build community, and know they can't get to where they're going alone.

Questions

1 How did it feel the last time I was celebrated?

2 Who am I most thankful for? When was the last time I told them?

3 Am I an (pick one):

☐ influencer

☐ leader

Your challenge.

Practice is everything. Make a list of three people around you who deserve to be celebrated, even if it's just in small ways.

Then, do it.

NOTES

I think the most important difference between leaders and influencers is their *intent*. To me, that's everything.

Influencers, or wannabe influencers, usually intend to gain a following and use it for personal benefit (typically by selling you something).

Leaders, on the other hand, have bigger, bolder aspirations. A leader's intent is to create some positive impact, and not just for themselves. There's an element of selflessness — they aim to build teams and communities. When we think

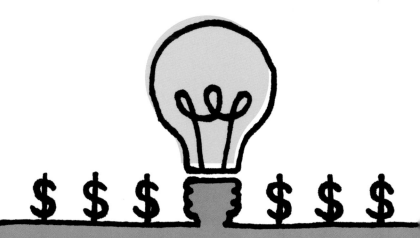

of great leaders, we don't consider their online following, the clothing they wear, or the cars they drive. (Elon Musk may be an exception because he *invented* his car.) Instead, we think about the tangible impact they have, the change they've caused, and the fact that the world is better because they're in it. Because of this, the world's greatest leaders also influence the most people.

So, what's your intent?

Here's a simple way to check yourself. Think about what you spend more time on each week: constructing tweets and plotting your next Instagram photo, or brainstorming creative ways to impact your community, celebrate others, and go out of your way to help people.

Your answer to that question shows what you actually value more: doing or talking, leadership or influence, legacy or likes.

WHAT'S HAPPENING?

4

WISH.
TALK.
DO.

Let me toss out a scenario: Say there's a dance or a party happening — some major social event. The way these things typically work is leaders create an event they hope can be fun for a lot of people. They recruit others to join their team and hold a meeting to organize it. They plan and execute everything — budget, venue, permissions, entertainment, lighting, decorations, promotion. Everything.

The leader works really hard. But no matter how well they do their job, they're just hoping the influencers — those kids who tend to dictate the high school's culture — show up or acknowledge the event online with a like or RSVP. *That's it*. The influencer can bless the leader's work with a stamp of approval within a half-second. Because if the influencers do any of these things, everyone else is more likely to follow suit.

We're all in that story somewhere: Some of us lead the party; some of us influence others to attend; and some of us are just part of the crowd.

Which role do you identify with? There's no right or wrong answer. The truth is, you're going to spend most of your life being all three. At times, we all lead (build our legacy). We all have moments where we influence those around us (build our likes). And there are times when we all ride the wave (click that "follow" button).

Sometimes we follow because we're inspired by a leader and believe in their cause. Sometimes it's because we're attracted to a certain influencer. And sometimes we follow because it just feels most comfortable. All of those reasons are totally natural, and they can even be healthy.

But when we follow because we don't feel qualified to lead, that's when I see a problem. It's a dangerous game convincing yourself you're not up to the task of leading: *I'm not pretty/trendy/smart/charismatic/_____ enough, so why even start?*

To me, that kind of thinking sounds like you're making excuses and not giving yourself a chance to find your voice or create your story.

You'll always be able to find an excuse not to do something.

But look back at the leaders you listed in Chapter Two. Those people who make a real difference in their communities and in the world all figured out how to fight past the urge to play it safe, or just click "like" all day.

You can be a leader too. It doesn't matter if you're the kid reading this only because your teacher assigned it, or if you're the kid who hates school and is counting down the days until you're outta there. You can lead in small moments at school just by kicking your effort or engagement into gear, even if you don't like the subject matter or the group you're working in. You lead when you stand up for people when no one else has the courage. You lead when you have an idea about who you want to be and start to chip away at it. **Leadership isn't about being in the spotlight or being the most popular. It's about how you do the small things.**

I know how tempting it can be to live only in that follower world. I've been there. By all accounts, I was average in high school. I came from an unremarkable family and spent most of my childhood with unremarkable aspirations. And then there's my name: Mike Smith. Literally, it's the fourth-most-common first name and most common last name in the United States. There are an estimated 40,000 other Mike Smiths in this country. (We could completely take over 20 towns the size of Imperial.)

I spent a lot of time following. But I also looked up to people who were doing cool stuff — musicians, artists, skateboarders, people who traveled the world. And at some point my senior year, I decided I wasn't going to let my grades, test scores, the town I grew up in, and definitely not my name stop me from living the life I wanted.

I was going to carve my own path.

Looking around at the friends, coaches, teachers, and community leaders I'd met, I realized being average — and being a follower — was a choice.

I've noticed there are three types of people in this world: those who wish, those who talk, and those who do.

Wishers: Your social media feed is filled with influencers, and you spend hours scrolling through profile after profile. You have a dream lifestyle, and you pray someone or something will walk into your life one day and magically make it happen. You spend much of your time wishing you could live in a different city, have a different body, change some part of your personality, or come from a different family. You're so wrapped up in wishing things could be different that you paralyze yourself and have trouble ever actually doing anything.

Talkers: Your feed is a mix of both influencers and leaders. You're all about telling others your plans, but they might seem skeptical you're ever actually going to execute them. You manage to get the same satisfaction out of talking about a future life as others get out of actually living one. You're super loud online, but when it comes to putting in the time and the work, you're drawn to making excuses and sometimes blame other people for why something didn't work out. (See also: social media complainers, who tweet all the time at brands, celebs, politicians, and famous people. They hit "send" and it's like they've accomplished something. They haven't.)

Doers: Your feed is filled with leaders. You put your head down to get to work. Rather than posting about what you want to do (or even what you're doing), you're striving to create something that makes a difference for you, and maybe even for those around you. Most of all, you're not concerned with what a few dozen kids from high school might think about you. You have a purpose, a passion, and you're fresh out of excuses. So you go out and you just *do*.

In my experience, it usually goes like this: **Leaders *do*; influencers *talk*; and followers *wish*.** Which of those types of people most often describes you? (And are you happy with your answer?)

We live in an age where talkers and wishers clog our feeds with words, memes, quotes, and GIFs focused on what they stand for and what's important to them. But it's rare when those sentiments make it past the "share" or "send" buttons on their phones and into their physical lives. **The one thing people who are truly changing the world have in common is that they *do something* about what they stand for.**

We all know being a doer is the most admirable of the three roles, so why do most of us live in the "wish" and "talk" camps? What's our excuse?

Sometimes our confidence or ambition has been threatened, like when parents tell kids they're not good enough, or that their dreams won't make for a "real career." Most of the time I think our excuse boils down to self-doubt and fear: We doubt we're qualified to actually do the thing we care so much about, or we fear others' judgement if we try and fail.

What about you? What's the excuse bouncing around inside your brain telling you not to try? Whose voice is in your head making you doubt yourself? Is it a parent, a bully, a boyfriend or girlfriend? We all have that voice we allow to tell us we can't do something, and too often, we let that outside voice become our own.

When we allow that to happen, we take *ourselves* out of the game! But our lives are too short for that. **We have a finite number of days here on this planet, and we don't get do-overs.** Your life is too important to waste a second listening to negative voices telling you what you can't do.

"Do things that are important to you. Keep giving. Givers are leaders, and there's enough room for all of us."

Jordin Sparks, singer/songwriter
from her episode of "The Harbor by Jostens"

When I have a new dream or idea — something I really want to try or create, or some risk I really want to take — I do this one simple activity:

1. Take a sheet of paper.

2. Draw a line down the middle.

3. On the left side, list all the things you're scared *might* happen if you fail: What could go wrong? What are you truly afraid of? What's holding you back? Be specific. Keep going until you can't think of any other potential fears or problems.

4. On the right side, list all the things that would happen if you succeeded and realized your dream: Who would it impact? How would your life and the lives of others be different? Where would you go? What would you experience? What new skills would you gain? How would those things impact your live moving forward?

Here's what you're usually going to find: The good list is going to outweigh the bad. Achieving something unique to you and your dreams is going to be worth the risk.

WHAT HAPPENS IF I	WHAT HAPPENS IF I
# FAIL?	# SUCCEED?
_____	_____
_____	_____
_____	_____
_____	_____
_____	_____
_____	_____
_____	_____
_____	_____
_____	_____

But you have to understand, **the world isn't going to do it for you.**

No one is going to magically walk into your life and just make "it" happen. Not your mom and dad. Not your teacher. *You* have to be the one who takes the chance for yourself, and I promise you this: When you do go for it, and I mean *truly go for it*, it won't matter if you win or lose. Pushing yourself to get over the fear of failing, or the fear of what someone else might think if you fail, is the biggest lesson to be learned. It makes you stronger immediately, and it makes striving for what you want a little easier each time until it becomes a natural part of what makes you, you.

All great leaders know their lives are not just about winning or creating something new. The life of a leader is about believing in yourself enough to conquer the doubters, haters, and the voices inside your head, even your own.

Questions

1   If I play it safe my whole life, who will I become?

2   Which do I spend more time thinking about: the impact people have on me, or the impact I can have on people?

3   Which question matters more to me: "How can I make someone else look better?" or "How can I make myself look better?"

Your challenge.

1. Do Mike's exercise.

2. Write out the words "WISH," "TALK," and "DO" on a sheet of paper. Identify a few areas in which you do these things.

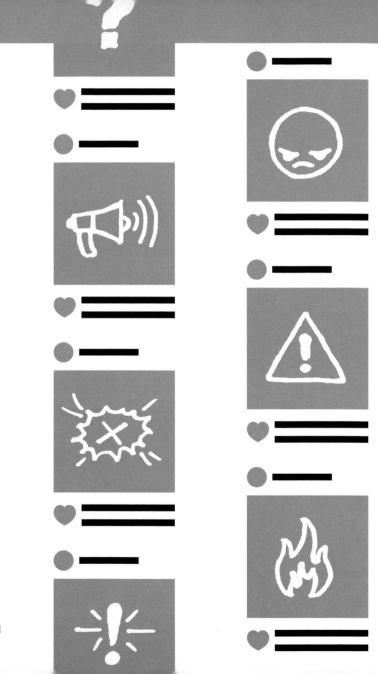

If your timeline looks anything like mine, it's filled with a lot of noise: people complaining about the political climate, activists pointing out hypocrisy, people tweeting at airlines or restaurants to criticize their service. Or it's a barrage of the latest memes, GIFs, or viral videos. It's influencers posting about products, musicians tweeting about their new song, or well-crafted tweets someone hopes will "break the internet" for a day or two.

I recently had a memorable conversation with a high school girl about feminism and the role social media plays in bringing awareness to it. She was incredibly vocal about her position, and I admired her willingness to take a stand on a tough issue at such a young age. We began talking about equal pay for women, the disparity between women who are teachers and men who hold the principal or superintendent jobs in a sector dominated by women. (The stats are truly staggering.) The conversation was engaging and enjoyable, but it took a serious turn when I asked her to show me her Twitter account.

She handed me her phone, and I noticed for every post she made about these subjects, she had as many or more disparaging tweets about other girls in her school. I started reading them out loud to her (as she cringed) and asked, "How can you use your account to empower and at the same time to devalue and talk trash?"

She didn't have a logical answer. I don't think she'd ever considered the inconsistency. Our conversation led to a simple takeaway:

Real impact isn't found online. It's found in the streets, in our schools, and in our communities.

Posting about issues doesn't solve them. It doesn't end homelessness or feed people. It doesn't build houses for people who need shelter or teach people to read. Those things take *doing*. If you have a following, I believe it's your duty to use it to help those in need. Awareness means nothing without action behind it.

So to the digital finger-pointers, the professional complainers, and the call-out kids: Please do yourself, your timeline, and your community a favor.

Stop tweeting about it, and start being about it.

scrolling through Instagram, sending snaps, watching Netflix or YouTube, or messaging friends. The average kid today gets their first smartphone when they're ten years old. (I was twenty.)

If you spend 6.5 hours a day on screens from, say, ninth grade until your five-year high school reunion, that comes to well over 20,000 hours of your young adult life. You don't have to be awesome at math to realize that's twice Gladwell's 10,000 hours spent consuming someone else's content instead of honing your own craft. Your high school years are hugely important for developing your passions, talents, and experiences. The habits — good and bad — you form in that time lay the foundation for the rest of your life.

If we spend so much time watching how others spend their time, how can we ever be truly great with our own?

Whether it's coding, graphic design, woodworking, stage choreography, or baking, true leaders have a craft. Any young person has the time to become an expert in one or two areas, but we've traded creation for consumption.

Let's try something: Pull out your phone. Go into settings > battery. At the bottom of the screen, you should see your battery usage for the last twenty-four hours. Write it down, and start paying attention to it. What apps take up most of your time? Be honest with yourself here for a minute: Where is your attention going? Are you scrolling through IG for hours on end, or reading tweet after tweet? Maybe you're one of those 250-snaps-a-day people. (Can't break your snap streak, right? Super important.)

Teachers, I don't want you to act as if you're innocent here either. You know what I'm talking about. Some of us adults are just as guilty of sinking hours into our screens: from Facebook to Pinterest, from *Words With Friends* to *Candy Crush*.

We all escape to our phones at times, but how many hours a day are we wasting by consuming and liking someone else's story instead of creating our own? Remember: **We prove our values through our time investments. The things we give attention to are the things that grow.**

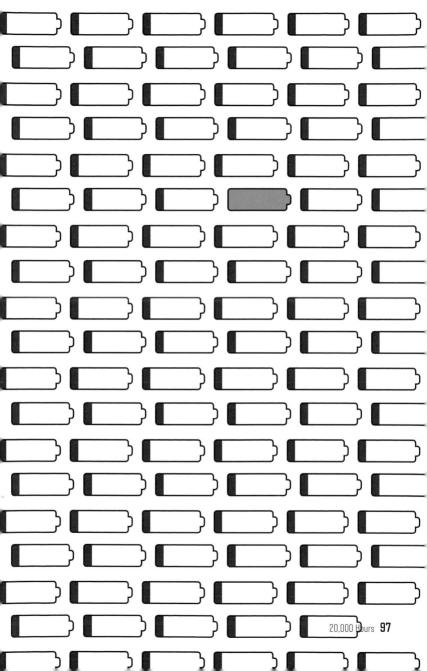

20,000 Hours **97**

> "People want to shine like Diddy but don't want to work like Puff. They wanna be the final product without the work put in, and it's impossible."

Quincy, musician/actor
from his episode of "The Harbor by Jostens"

Let's be real: Is social media a good place to invest your thousands of hours? How much of the stuff you see on your phone do you forget about within a month? Or how about within a week? A day? An hour? How much of it do you not even care about *while you're looking at it*? We all know on some level that the vast majority of what we consume via our phones has no real impact on our lives.

So what are you spending your time on?

When I speak with older generations, I hear time and time again the regrets people have about not investing more time into what truly mattered in their lives. They wish they could go back and commit to the pursuits they were passionate about, enjoy more moments with their loved ones, and create stories they'd never forget.

One thing that's true about this world is it doesn't matter where you come from, how much money your parents have, how tall, pretty, or charismatic you are — **we all have the same number of hours in a day. You cannot buy more time.**

But you can start making your time count today.

What if all you did was cut your screen time in half?

Think about what would happen if we spent 3.25 hours each day creating, rather than consuming. That's 195 minutes a day to improve your skills at taking photos, editing videos, playing tennis, dancing, writing, or painting. If you knew you could achieve excellence in one of these areas, how different would your habits be? How much more confidence would you have? Imagine if you cut down your screen time for nine years and gave yourself 10,000 free hours — how incredible would you be at the thing you say you're passionate about?

No leaders excel at their crafts simply because they are naturally gifted. They may have started with some natural ability, but they worked hard to become masters of the little things — the fundamentals. **It really boils down to how they spent all their available hours.**

So many young people today spend those hours consuming content, paying attention to everyone else's lives, and trying to mimic influencers. They miss out on being great at something, and they forego all the rewards that come with it.

So what about you — if you could get back the countless hours you've given to your phone, mindlessly scrolling through stuff that *truly does not matter*, what would you be good at? What craft would you have dialed in? What's that skill you've always wished you had?

What's the thing you're deciding *not* to become great at?

Questions

1 How do I feel about the fact that I spend thousands of hours (over the course of my life) on my phone?

2 What's something I've always wanted to do but haven't because I claim to have no time?

3 What are some areas of my life where I know I spend empty time?

Your
challenge.

1. For one week, force yourself to work on your craft for 2.5 hours before you're allowed to log in.

2. Keep track of your hours on social vs. your hours working on your craft.

NEW POST

Kids email and DM me so frequently, asking how to start nonprofits or how to become speakers, that I've had to create a separate email account just to answer the same two or three questions. As I've corresponded with students, I'm surprised to find how little time they've spent actually researching the thing they want to do or the people who do it well. There seems to be a divide between *what* kids want to be and the people they follow.

In the same way what you eat and drink affects your body, if you want maximum results mentally, you have to feed your mind with information that enlightens or pushes you — not distracts you from your goals. That might sound cheesy and obvious, but stop and really think about it for a moment: *How are you feeding your mind?*

For instance, if you want to be a photographer, are you following (and studying) great photographers whose work inspires and challenges you? If you want to start a nonprofit, are you following people who've actually done it? No matter what you want to be, the internet is flooded with profiles and resources that can show you how to create and grow your passion.

If you're interested in creating your story and building your legacy, take a hard look at who and what is filling your timeline.

Ask yourself:

- Is what I'm paying attention to helping me be a better me? A kinder, more authentic version of myself? Or is it causing me to be jealous or envious of others?

- Does my timeline make me more positive or negative? Is it filled with things that build me up, or does it tear down my opinion of myself and others?

- Am I letting content take up space in my brain that subtracts from my happiness or divides my effectiveness? Are the things I'm filling my timeline with adding to or multiplying my world?

There is only so much room in our brains, so let's fill it with the things that make us better students, friends, and community members. The next time you click that "follow" button, remember, *if it's in our timelines, it's in our minds.*

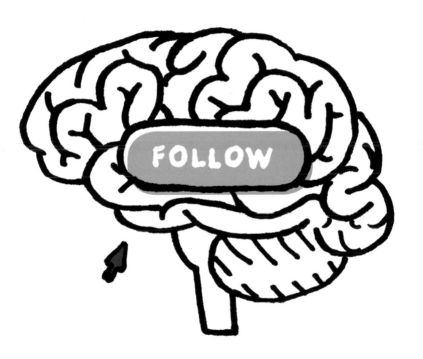

NOTES

6

STORIES,
NOT
STUFF

In the last few years alone, I've spoken in front of well over one million students from thousands of different schools across the country and the world. For every ten days you were in school last year, I was in school for eight of them. (I can't even quantify the number of lunchroom chocolate milks and chicken patties I've consumed.)

Before and after I speak, I spend time walking down the halls, talking to kids in classes and sometimes just hanging out. And I see a lot of the same *stuff*. It doesn't matter if the school is urban or rural, public or private, homogenous or diverse; students all talk about the same stuff, wear the same stuff, and dance to the same stuff. They even try to be identified as unique by doing or owning the same stuff. Countless times, I've seen a new trend — a phrase, dance, hairstyle, GIF, meme, social craze — take the country by storm, coast to coast, almost overnight. I'm talking from fidget spinners to "Juju On That Beat," from the resurrection of socks and sandals (I still don't get that one) to the evolution of the duckface selfie.

One of the most interesting revelations from my six-year journey into the halls of high schools has been that no matter how hard everyone is trying to be different, they all end up doing basically the same stuff.

It's as if everyone is being the same kind of "unique."

Not surprisingly, teens today spend *three times* as much money on clothes, shoes, electronics, and entertainment as on food. Trust me, your stuff doesn't actually make you special — it's your creativity, your personality, and your drive that separate you from others. But we've all bought into that first idea. We've purchased (or wished we could purchase) that thing we thought was going to make us stand out, be special, be different. It was that way when I was a kid; it's that way today; it will be that way until the end of time.

The real danger in caring deeply about material possessions is when they start to become ways to identify, categorize, and even judge people. You start playing the comparison game, believing someone is more or less valuable based on what they have, and not who they are. The desire for stuff only creates this feeling that the more you get, the more important you are.

*H*ave you ever thought about your funeral? Be real now. We all have.

We think: Who would be there? What would they say about me? What will be written on my tombstone?

Do you think anyone is going to say a single word about the brand of shoes or phone you had in high school? With your family and friends gathered around celebrating your life, will anyone reference how many Instagram followers you had? Not a chance. They'll talk about the person you were and the stories and adventures you shared. They'll recount the times you proved you were a good friend and the times you were there when they needed you most. They'll speak to how you made them feel, and how you impacted or inspired them. Their stories will be about why they loved *you* ... not your stuff.

"I realized I had to start being comfortable with the uncomfortable. I had to step out of anything that I was doing — I had to share my story so that other people felt like they could come forward and share their story."

Davey Muise, musician/speaker
from his episode of "The Harbor by Jostens"

Q: You know why you never see a U-Haul attached to a hearse?

A: Because you can't take it with you.

That stuff you accumulate, stress about getting, or hope to have someday won't remotely matter at the end of your life. Only the people in your life will.

The question of what's truly important is a fundamental issue in our lives, because the fact is, we're all gonna die. It's not a question of if; it's a question of when. Thinking about that reality always makes me ask myself, *"What do I want to be remembered for?"*

If your answer to that question is anything like mine, it has nothing to do with stuff. If we agree that's true, why don't we spend more time living for the stories told at our funerals than for the superficial stuff we can buy or gawk at online?

My high school was no different than yours: The easiest way to stand out was with stuff. But my family couldn't afford a lot of those things, and I always loved going against the status quo, so I found myself investing more in stories I could live out, and later tell.

With that in mind, my senior year of high school, I sat down with a few friends and **wrote a list of things we wanted to *do* before we graduated high school.**

This list wasn't mind-blowing. It included things like trying to break the Guinness World Record for throwing a grape the farthest and someone catching it in their mouth, or tossing and catching an egg over the longest distance without breaking it. We built bonfires, went camping, climbed our town's water tower. We experienced activities we always thought would be fun, exciting, or even just interesting. Some of these turned out incredibly rewarding (like making cookies for the local nursing home), some not so much (like using a car to pull an old bathtub across a field, while we surfed it). Along the way, we challenged ourselves, expanded our life stories, gained skills, and grew friendships. We learned how to become doers, and we

ADVENTURE LOG

- [ ] _____
- [ ] _____
- [ ] _____
- [ ] _____
- [ ] _____
- [ ] _____
- [ ] _____
- [ ] _____
- [ ] _____
- [ ] _____
- [ ] _____
- [ ] _____
- [ ] _____
- [ ] _____

built a ton of memories we still talk about when we're together.

We didn't make this list to become known, to stage a perfect photo, or for the likes. (We didn't have anywhere to post that stuff, and we weren't competing with anyone for the best adventure.) We did it because we truly wanted to *live* these moments: the harshness of failing and the joy of completing something new. We did it just for us, for our own adventure, for our own stories.

I *realized when I invested in stories, I began to have a much deeper impact* — not just on my own life but also on those around me. And it felt like positive things began to snowball.

As I spent less time complaining about growing up in a small town, and more time being creative with my time, I increasingly discovered new passions, passions that turned into skills. The more adventures I took, the more good habits I developed.

I think that's what high school is all about: building habits, pushing yourself, breaking outside the mold of

CHASE
STORIES

NOT
STUFF

what's expected of you. It's about beginning your story.

Living for stories is one of my core beliefs to this day. I still have a list of challenges I'm constantly pushing to accomplish — I call it my Adventure Log. It includes things like: skateboarding across America; surfing, skating, and snowboarding in the same 24-hour period; going thirty days with no technology; fixing up my old truck; creating my own high school; and even running for president. (Look for me in 2024.)

When you invest in stories, you give the people around you permission to dream differently.

That's leadership. That's building a legacy.

When I consider leaders I admire (including those in high school halls), I recognize two fundamental qualities they all share: the willingness to dream differently and the commitment to invest in stories, not stuff.

Questions

1 What's my favorite story or adventure I've experienced? Why does it hold a special and permanent place in my memory?

2 What are three things I've always wanted to do but haven't for whatever reason?

3 What stops me from living a life full of adventure?

4 What am I investing in? (What do my Friday nights look like?)

5 What do I want to be remembered for?

Your challenge.

Create your own adventure log (with friends or by yourself). Write down all the things you've always wanted to do, and get after it.

WHAT'S ON YOUR MIND?

Tell me if this sounds familiar: You're scrolling through your phone, jumping from Instagram to Twitter, over to Snapchat, back to Instagram, and then it's off to YouTube, and back again to Snapchat to see if you have any new snaps. Thirty minutes turns into an hour, then into two, and eventually you're so far down the rabbit hole on Instagram you would have to hit "back" so many times to return to your profile that it's easier to just close the app and start over.

We've all been there, right? In the blink of an eye, a giant chunk of our day is gone, and we have nothing to show for it. It might feel like we just ate a whole sleeve of Oreos without thinking, or binge-watched an entire season of television just because the next episode was ... there.

But what drives that scrolling and tapping through apps? Does it come from a different place than gobbling cookies or Netflix episodes? Deep down, do we feel like we *have* to be on our apps?

So in an experiment to see if this obsession with social media is more of an addiction, I decided to challenge thousands of kids across the country to delete all the social apps from their phones and do a digital detox for thirty days.

I wanted to show people not only how much time we spend consuming content but also how much time we would have to create if we weren't so distracted.

Most of the students I challenged didn't even try the detox. Of those who actually attempted it, fewer than half made it 30 days. Most quit within the first two weeks.

Most kids told me they didn't complete the challenge because they couldn't give up their snap streaks, or they had no other way of communicating with their friends. Here are some quotes from the brave kids who at least *tried*:

Succeeded:

"I felt like I was disconnected, but my parents liked it more. When my mom talked to me, I would actually answer."

"At first I was kind of bored, but I've actually gotten a lot of homework done. But at the same time, I feel really disconnected. Like, prom was last night, and I don't even know what everybody else looked like."

Tried but failed:

"I failed right away. I downloaded Snapchat right away. I made it for one hour. I was going to tell people I was going to delete it, and then I just ... did it again."

"I redownloaded it, because my friend committed to a school for soccer. I wanted to recognize her, so I thought I'd just post this one thing, but once I got a little taste of it, I couldn't stop."

had one *particularly* interesting conversation with an 18-year-old who completed the challenge.

How did it feel not having access to your social media for a month?

Mike Smith

It was hard. It was honestly way harder than I thought it would be.

Zoey

And what made it so hard to unplug?

I hated feeling like I was missing out on something. It felt like there were things going on that I didn't get to see or didn't know about until way after they happened. And that's the main way I communicate with my friends during the day. We mostly just text and snap all day.

Did you feel like you were able to just be you at all, like you were able to just unplug and focus on yourself instead of what everyone else was doing?

Yeah, of course. You realize right away how much time you spend on your phone, or when you're with a group of people and everyone around you is on their phone and you're not. It's crazy how many times I reached for my phone. I unlocked it and tried to open up my apps, but they weren't there. I definitely realized I'm addicted to my phone, for sure.

Zoey

What are you looking at when you're looking at your phone? If all your classmates are in school at the same time you are, what could there possibly be to look at?

Mike Smith

I follow a ton of blogs and lifestyle pages. I look at what other girls are wearing or how they did their hair or makeup. I follow a ton of those "influencer" pages on Instagram and Snapchat.

So do you compare yourself to those girls, then, if you follow them?

Mike Smith

Yeah, of course. We all compare ourselves to the people we follow and look at.

Zoey

So when you couldn't look at your apps for 30 days, do you think you felt more secure about yourself or less secure?

And then this response blew my mind.

I felt way more insecure without my apps than with them.

Wait, I'm confused. How is that possible?

When I post a cute pic of myself, I know I'll get 250-300 people to tell me they "like" me. All my friends will comment on how cute I look, and that makes me feel good. When I didn't have my Instagram, those interactions didn't happen for a month.

Zoey

That makes sense. So what feels better though: if someone tells you on Instagram they think you look cute, or if someone tells you in person?

Mike Smith

It always feels better in person, for sure. It just doesn't happen very often. And for sure not 250 times a day, haha.

Do you compliment your friends every day? Like, if we know it feels better to be complimented in person, do you make that a priority?

Not as much as I should, no.

Zoey

Isn't that what we want though, that more personal, real connection, rather than just a post on our pic or timeline?

Mike Smith

It depends, I guess.

On what?

Who the compliment is coming from.

What if it was me? What if I was to compliment you on your outfit? Where would you rather that happen: in person or on your picture?

On my picture, for sure!

Zoey

Wait, why?

Mike Smith

Because then everyone would see it. If you just said it to my face, I couldn't show that to anyone, and no one would know it happened. If you commented on my pic or timeline, I would screen grab it and send that to my friends.

So you would trade the more meaningful conversations for one that you could show your friends online?

If it was a compliment from someone famous or influential or popular, yeah, for sure.

I left that interaction with more questions than answers.

What's the tipping point when online kudos become more valuable than thoughtful, face-to-face praise? Is it two likes? Is it ten? Is it 250?

Do we now live in a space where the predominant currency has become likes rather than genuine human interaction? *Have we traded authentic communication for the "like" button?*

I understand we all want to feel connected. At school, work, home, and online, we all crave some level of social interaction with others. In fact, a growing body of research shows this desire is actually as basic a need as food, water, and shelter. Social media keeps us in touch with people we'd never otherwise see, and it helps show us new and interesting cultural conversations. I'm not saying it has no value.

But don't we also want *real* connection? If your social media presence doesn't reflect the truest version of yourself — the good, bad, and the ugly — those likes aren't real anyway, right? And let's be honest, whose social profiles aren't curated to make them look as good as possible? Yours is. Mine is. Of course, we all try to paint ourselves in the best possible light.

We know a lot *about* the people we follow online — their vacations, successes, and interests. But we've all had that awkward moment when we run into these people in real life and realize we don't *really* know them.

Social media culture also makes me wonder if we have become addicted to attention. Are we so hungry for instant gratification that we're always working to impress a digital audience? If so, what is the cost? If our 20,000 hours are being spent trying to be seen, appreciated, or connected, what are we missing out on in the real world that might fulfill us in more meaningful and permanent ways?

I would offer you this thought: Take some time to unplug. Maybe it's a day, a weekend, a week, a month — hell, even a year. Don't do it because constantly being connected is necessarily bad or wrong — I'm not saying that's the case.

Do a digital detox to learn what matters more to you. Where do you actually get your validation? What is the currency you care about most? I don't think there's a wrong answer either way. But I do think one of those currencies leads to building a legacy — the other, well, you get the idea.

"What if we stopped focusing so much on how many Instagram followers we had and put our phones down long enough so that we could see and really know the people that we pass in the hallways every single day?"

Kat Harris, photographer/blogger
from her episode of "The Harbor by Jostens"

NEW POST

7

WHEN NO ONE IS LOOKING

I truly believe *anyone* can become a leader. Whether you've been wishing, talking, following, or influencing, you have what it takes to become a leader. You just have to make the decision to do it.

But if you're trying to become a true leader, your intentions need to be pure. The role of leader is not for the selfish.

I once spoke at a very affluent school in California, where students were expected to excel and achieve. This school and its surrounding community were massively proud of their academics and activities. It wasn't the most diverse school I've ever been to, and its student body was extremely segregated by interests, beliefs, and socioeconomic differences. Like most schools, it had its cliques — football players, drama department, skaters/surfers, LGBTQ+, water polo kids, debate squad. It seemed as if everyone had their own lane, and everyone kind of accepted that's the way it was.

After speaking, I walked into this school's cafeteria to snag my complimentary chicken nuggets and chocolate milk. And in this place, where everyone goes to the same spot every day to eat and talk about the same things with the same people, something was slightly "off."

I weaved my way through backpacks on the floor and through round tables filled with students talking, texting, snappin', and 'grammin', and I headed to eat lunch with the special needs kids. (If you have ever worked with me at your school, you know I do this every lunchtime, everywhere I go. Reaching out to students with disabilities is a huge priority for me.)

But on this particular day, my normal lunchtime crew looked very different. The cheerleaders were mixed in with special needs students — laughing, eating, just hanging out. I paused for a moment before I sat down to really assess what I was looking at. In my six years of speaking at schools across the country, this was a first.

Now, I have met so many amazing students who spend time with their peers who have special needs. There are some excellent programs and schools that work incredibly hard to be inclusive of everyone.

DID YOU REALLY
HELP SOMEONE
IF YOU DIDN'T
POST IT ON INSTAGRAM?

But this situation seemed different.

I struck up a convo with everyone. We started with small talk, and I asked a whole list of questions. We went back and forth about our favorite bands, movies, and classes. Lunch was awesome — the cheerleaders had genuine relationships and connections with these students, and it was clear to me this is what they do every day.

When lunch finished, I tossed my empty carton into the overflowing cafeteria trash can and pulled aside the cheerleader who seemed to be the leader of the pack. I asked her something like, "Was this a program your school implemented? How did this happen? When did this start? Do you get some sort of community service hours?"

And her response floored me.

She said she wanted to be a special ed teacher, so she spends as much time as she can around those students at her own school. She started eating lunch with them every day back during her freshman year. She happened to be "that cheerleader" who everyone

"Once you have the platform to (give back), you have to do it.

"You only have a small window to be great ... You have to take advantage of the opportunity."

Von Miller, NFL linebacker and Super Bowl 50 MVP
from his episode of "The Harbor by Jostens"

144

followed and who was incredibly influential in her school. So her fellow classmates, naturally, joined her. Fast forward to her senior year, and there's an entire school rallying around this community of kids that is so often socially isolated.

The cheerleader told me about the special needs prom the school hosts. (Students with disabilities can go to the all-school prom if they want, but that environment doesn't always make for a fun night.) She described how hard she worked to get them involved in after-school activities as well — bringing them to football games and musicals, spending time with them playing video games on the weekends. She said the school's leadership makes sure the entire student body is involved in everything, and these students should be no different.

She made ensuring these kids were truly part of the school her top priority during those four years. Honestly, listening to her talk with such passion about this cause choked me up. (It still does when I think about it.)

I asked her teachers about her — what's her angle? The response was the same, across the board: Her sole motivation was to positively impact those kids. She didn't care who saw what she was doing, or whether anyone came with her. She did it because it was the right thing to do.

She had realized her influence. But instead of using that power to grow her social media following or to win prom queen, she put it to work making others happier, putting the spotlight on them. And people followed.

She moved from influencer to leader by making small, simple sacrifices that put others first. In the end, she influenced an entire school to be kinder and more compassionate.

She took her influence and created a legacy.

I believe we reveal our true selves when we think no one is watching.

My first semester of college, my basketball coach asked me what I wanted to get out of my experience at the school. I looked him in the eye and answered honestly: "I want to get my degree, and I want to help people."

He looked at me with a straight face and replied, "If you want to help people, get in my truck."

My initial thought was: "My mom warned me about people like you, HA!" But I quickly realized he was serious. So I hopped in the front seat of his pickup, and he drove me a couple miles from campus to a highway bridge. We walked together until we were standing next to its railing. Pointing below the bridge, he said, "If you want to help people, start with them."

I looked down and saw what was clearly a makeshift community of homeless people. Coming from a small town, my interactions with this population were very limited. But I realized this was my moment to not just "wish" or "talk" about helping someone, but actually follow through.

I walked under that bridge and introduced myself to the first person I saw. I reached out to shake the man's hand and said, "My name's Mike. How can I help?" The man proceeded to tell me his name, where he was from, and how he ended up homeless. We talked for ten or fifteen minutes about his life and his journey, and then he looked at me and said, "All I need right now is a pair of socks."

Not fully understanding why he needed socks so badly, I asked him. He took off his shoes and showed me his feet, which were covered in blisters and callouses because he had been wearing the same socks for weeks straight. He explained he could get food and other clothing, but getting socks was the most difficult. He said when it rained or snowed, or his feet got sweaty, his socks would never dry. As a result, his feet were destroyed.

I instantly thought, "OK, I gotta get this dude some socks."

That's exactly what I did. Not having that many pairs of my own to give, and with hardly any money in my bank account, I did the only thing I could think of: I snagged as many free pairs from our basketball team's equipment room as I could carry. I went back under that bridge and started passing out socks.

I didn't just do it once, and I didn't tell everyone I was doing it. I quietly spent time every week heading under that bridge and handing out whatever I could get my hands on. There was no post on social media — no perfectly crafted status about my experience for the world to read. It was just me, some socks, and my hope that something so simple could make even the smallest bit of difference in someone's life.

It made me realize truly helping people could be easy. It didn't require millions of dollars or a huge organization. You didn't have to have an organized group (all rocking matching T-shirts) who'd spent hundreds of hours planning. Often, what people need most are the small things. A group of likeminded, selfless helpers formed over time, and soon we were regularly handing out socks, spending time with the people under the bridge, and actually *listening* to their stories. These little things make people feel human and have a way of giving them their dignity. Sometimes you're not just improving a circumstance; sometimes **you're helping the soul.**

The people in the makeshift camp specifically wanted white socks. And why? Because they look new when they're clean. It really is the little things.

It was just a simple act of kindness and love I performed because **helping people matters most when no one else is looking.**

So if you're like me, and all you want to do when you "grow up" is help people, here's some advice: **Don't do it for the pic, your resume, community service hours, or because it's trendy to give back. Do it for them.** Do it because you genuinely care. Do it because you're a leader, and you want to leave the place you're in better than you found it.

If you're not sure where to begin, look around you. Who's nearby who needs help? Reach out your hand, and introduce yourself.

Start there.

Questions

1 How am I using my influence or potential?

2 When was the last time I volunteered because I wanted to, not for any other reason?

3 What cause or social issue matters most to me? What can I do to help, even something small?

4 Do the influencers or leaders I most look up to give back?

5 What matters more to me: making an impact, or having people know I'm making an impact?

Your challenge.

Simple:

Help someone, and don't tell a soul about it.

WHAT'S HAPPENING?

Ready to start building your legacy but not sure about the first step? Here are some practical ideas to get you going:

- Eat lunch with the special needs class.

- Take a kid who struggles socially under your wing.

- Be quick to celebrate and compliment others.

- Show up when leaders work hard to plan an event. If you know people are influenced by you, you have a responsibility to support worthwhile causes and endeavors.

- If you play football, go to a band concert (or two — they show up for you).

- Brainstorm an idea for a business with your friends. Start it, and see if you can make money.

- Choose a charity or a community need that connects with your heart (research if you aren't sure). Google fundraiser ideas, and organize one to support your chosen cause.

- Audit the list of people and brands you follow, and ask yourself if each one is making you better or making you bitter. Then, purge that list.

- Go back to your elementary or middle school and thank a coach or teacher who impacted you. Tell them why.

- Thank your school's janitors in a creative way. They bust their butts, and it often goes unnoticed.

- Create your own Adventure Log, or challenge your friends to do something epic.

- Try out for a sport or school activity you've never done before.

- What's the one thing you're most afraid of? Force yourself to do or face it.

- Donate money to a kid overseas, or support your school's back-to-school drive or backpack program. (If you don't have something like that at your school, start it.)

- Sign up for a 5K or mud run. Get some friends to do it with you, and try to surprise yourself by going farther or faster than you predicted you could.

- Exercise. We all need to do that a little more.

- If you see a kid walking home from school and they're looking a little beat, offer them a ride.

- Create anonymous thank you cards and give them to people you see doing kind things. Don't tell anyone. Just do it for them.

- Shut off your radio, close Spotify, and listen to a podcast or two about a subject that interests you.

- Do something difficult: Give away a bunch of your clothing to someone who could use it. Go without shoes, or fast for twenty-four hours. Digital Detox for forty-eight hours.

8

SHUT UP
AND
LEAD

In every job I've ever had, I've felt a desire to make a difference but also do things my own way. (That's probably why I never held down a full-time job for more than two years until I was 25.)

My experience bringing socks to homeless people during college inspired me to become a street outreach worker in Lincoln, Nebraska. My goal was to help kids get off the street and turn their lives around.

It was an awesome job, and I felt like I was helping create some real change for people. But despite how fulfilling it was at times, my position was funded through a government grant, so it involved a ton of administration and bureaucracy. The formal job description, rules, and checks and balances all seemed to be getting in the way of my ability to actually *help* people.

I wanted the freedom to think outside the box, but my attempts to apply creativity to the services we provided were usually met with "no."

I felt like I was missing something.

During my time doing street outreach, I realized **kids all just need three basic things: a place to go, something to do, and people who care about them.**

When I looked around at my community, I saw lots of productive things for kids to do, that is, if they played sports or were really focused on school activities. And there were many organizations and people who genuinely worked hard to help young people. But I didn't see a place where kids who grew up like me — lovers of counterculture, like music, skating, or art — could feel at home. I didn't see a place where kids could feel accepted and encouraged to open up if they had issues at home, or were picked on in school, or lived in a shelter. I didn't see a place where those kids could feel connected and empowered.

I imagined a place young people who were at risk or on the fringe would feel comfortable calling their own. I imagined a place where kids who were a lot like I was — the creatives, the outliers, the misfits — could feel part of something bigger than themselves. I imagined a place that didn't exist.

So I decided to create it — an indoor skate park — a place for "those kids" to go.

I was still working the government-funded job, and I hoped my employer would be as excited as I was about my vision [*take a warning from Chapter Three*] and would want to create this space together. So I scheduled a meeting to pitch my idea to the outreach facility's leadership.

But I also decided I was creating this space with or without them. The night before the meeting, I wrote two documents: the plan to create the skate park and my letter of resignation. I told myself, no matter how my bosses responded to my pitch, I was walking out of that office with only one sheet of paper.

I left the room with my plan.

It was a big risk to quit a comfortable, fulfilling job to forge my own path. I didn't have the resources I needed to start this thing, and I certainly didn't have the experience. But I knew this was my chance to create my legacy — the thing I would be remembered for, the opportunity to leave a lasting mark on my community, the accomplishment they *would* talk about after I'm long gone.

"There's so much pressure to be the one thing, right?

"Curiosity is so vital to discovering maybe not just the one thing, but the four things, the five things.

"And if you live your life led by your curiosity, I think you can experience way more than just believing or buying into that idea that you only have to do one thing with your life."

Johan Khalilian, author/actor/speaker
from his episode of "The Harbor by Jostens"

It was my chance to go beyond wishing and talking and actually *do* the thing I said I was passionate about.

In February 2010, I Googled "how to start a nonprofit" and simply followed the instructions to register the organization, create a board of directors, and form articles of incorporation. With a staggering amount of help from a ton of friends, we used recycled ramps and barnwood to build a small, rather sketchy indoor skate park. We covered every inch of the place in graffiti, and that November, we opened the doors to The Bay.

I wasn't the best at any of the skills required for that space to open. I wasn't the best skater. I wasn't the best at construction. I wasn't the best at creating operating systems to make a nonprofit run smoothly — on and on and on.

At first, I faced a lot of skepticism, and even hate, from the outside world. Many in my state's core skateboarding scene didn't respect me. (Plenty still don't.) I heard all kinds of naysaying, both online and to my face. People told me I wasn't qualified. People flat-out told me they were rooting for me to fail.

For a while, I started to believe they might be right. There was a moment early on when I almost let self-doubt about not being the best stop me. But I took the risk. I told myself it didn't matter what people said. I knew how to work hard and how to celebrate others. I pushed through all the negativity, the criticism, and the lack of faith.

In 2010, I didn't have a massive following. I didn't have thousands of followers online, or famous skateboarders helping me, or shout-outs from celebrities. All I

I'm not here to be average.
I'm here to be awesome.

had was work ethic and a burning passion to create something bigger than myself.

Looking back, I realize five things were key to me going beyond wishing and talking, and actually creating my dream:

1. I surrounded myself with people who were more talented than I was every step of the way. From better skaters and artists to better money and time managers, I built a team of people that was collectively better than me in all the areas I needed support. And when the skate park started becoming successful, I didn't take the credit for it — I made it about *us*, not me.

2. After I built a team and started celebrating others, followers came and the world started to notice. That's when we took that little skate park and grew it into a massive warehouse that engages, educates, and provides necessary services to people in ways I never would have imagined. My team has dared to dream differently, and we have made a genuine impact on our city that will be felt — through the kids we help — for decades.

3. I was genuinely curious and asked tough questions. I had to be willing to humble myself and recognize I didn't have all the answers (and that I still don't). Even more importantly, I had to be open to getting tough answers in response to my questions. I had to listen to criticism and hard advice with an open mind.

4. I used these advisors as mentors. People willing to help you navigate opportunities and obstacles add tremendous value to your life and your story. From business people to nonprofit founders, I've invited countless people from multiple backgrounds to coffee so I can pick their brains, and so they can speak truth to me. The best part is, I've built wonderful friendships through these exchanges.

5. Finally, I knew I had to work harder than anyone around me, which is a principle I live by to this day. If you are the hardest-working person on your team, at your job, in your school, or wherever you end up, people will notice — and opportunity will follow.

If you walked into The Bay today, you would see a 33,000-square-foot warehouse in one of Lincoln's most impoverished neighborhoods that we renovated into a skate park, craft coffee shop, all-ages concert venue, and drop-in center for at-risk youth. We created a place where kids who love skating, art, and music can feel at home and thrive.

THE FUTURE

BELONGS

TO THE

MISFITS

We built The Bay as a team — and I'm not just talking about the walls, ramps, stage, and coffee bar. We built a culture and a community where kids are encouraged to lead and to be free with their own version of the attitude and spirit that built The Bay.

Here's the deal: The world wants you to find your thing. Honestly, it needs you to. And so do I. So it's time to get started.

An idea without a plan stays an idea. An idea with action becomes real. So put your idea on paper. Write out a plan, and do something small every day to keep pushing yourself, step by step, toward your goal.

Find a pursuit that makes your heart pound when you think about doing it for the rest of your life.

Find a problem you would give up everything to solve, and spend your life trying to solve it.

Sacrifice your time to chase your purpose or passion.

Push yourself to stop being like everyone around you, or what everyone expects you to be. Surprise yourself.

At some point, you have to stop renting your life and go own it. Don't hang out in the realm of "what if." Commit to your ideas and dreams, and fight for them in reality. Trust yourself to go all-in and learn some lessons in the process.

That's when you'll start to impact everything you touch.

That's when you'll find out what makes you, you. That's when you'll start to leave your legacy.

Questions

1 If I could do the last two years differently, what would I do? Who would I be?

2 What gives me energy? What makes me feel alive? Do I have a passion?

3 What's my thing?

4 What's stopping me from finding my thing or going out and trying to do it?

Your
challenge.

This should be a big one: Decide what you're going to do, create, and become. Write it down; put it on your mirror; tag me in the photo; tell your mom, gf, bf, or bff.

Make a plan and take one step each day closer to who it is you want to become.

Follow people who are doing what you want to do, and ask them to coffee. Be relentless about asking "how" and "what" they did to get where they are. Buy a book or two, download podcasts, watch documentaries or films — research and live what you've chosen to be about.

Google every question you could possibly have. Never stop asking questions.

Never stop.

ACKNOWLEDGMENTS

First and foremost, thanks to my wife, Amber — not just for letting me write this book while on vacation, but for being down to live this crazy thing we call life together. Love ya, Ber. • Thanks to my fam — Mom, Pops, Jessi, Katie, and Joey — for inspiring so many of the things I do. Love you, crazies. • Thanks to Andrew "Scoop" Norman for never turning down an opportunity to do something insane with me: from skating across Nebraska (on two days notice) to agreeing to help write this book ... in sixty days. Love ya, bud. • Thanks to my crew, Drew, Ruckus, Dingo, Nick Gross, EJay, Hansen, Alex, Fish, Ronnie, and the folks at ROROflix for all the late notices, late nights, and early mornings. Thanks for dealing with my ridiculous ideas, antics, and rants, and for being there when I need you most. • Thanks to my Jostens family for believing in me and my ideas to make the world better: one chapter, one stage, one video at a time. • Thanks to my Bay family for working so hard to make my silly passion something worth writing about in a book. You guys amaze me with your talents, grit, and love for the work we do. • Thanks to Chance, Quentin, and Ben for making this book read and look as if I know what I'm doing. We literally couldn't have made this happen without your hard work. • Thanks to all the guests from "The Harbor by Jostens" quoted in this book: Kelsea Ballerini, Azie Tesfai, Scott Backovich, Jordin Sparks, Quincy, Davey Muise, Kat Harris, Von Miller, and Johan Khalilian. I deeply appreciate your precious time and valuable insights. • To all you misfits, outliers, rule breakers, and crazy ones who have been with me on the journey: Thank you. Truly. • And let us all remember: The future belongs to the misfits.

— *Mike Smith*

Thank you, Angie (and Townsend), for believing in this journey of ours. I love you both to the moon and back. • Thanks, Mike, for never forgetting where you came from, and for making those of us around you better. • Thanks, Chance, for your trust, and otherworldly writing talent. • Thanks, Quentin and Ben, for all your hard (handsome) work. • Thanks to my Norman, Yerger and Clouatre family for your love and influence. • Thanks to my Hear Nebraska family, for all your faith, hustle, and sweat. Thanks to my mentors: John H., Dave P., Aaron S., Kendra I., Steve P., Marjorie M., Craig M. and Tim M. among them.

— *Andrew Norman*

CREDITS

PHOTOS

ILLUSTRATIONS